NATIONAL GEOGRAPHIC

WORLD HISTORY 3500–1000 B.C.

The First Civilizations

PICTURE CREDITS
Cover Bill Ellzey/National Geographic Image Collection; pages 1, 3 top right, 8, 49 Scala/Art Resource, NY; pages 3 top left, 22 right, 29, 30, 31 top Erich Lessing/Art Resource, NY; pages 3 bottom left, 50, 52 James L. Stanfield/National Geographic Image Collection; page 3 bottom right Gianni Dagli Orti/Corbis; pages 4–5, 9 middle, 35, 36, 37, 54–55 Kenneth Garrett/National Geographic Image Collection; page 6 Adam Woolfitt/Corbis; page 9 top Topham/The Image Works; page 9 bottom Nik Wheeler/Corbis; pages 10–11 Thomas Blackshear/National Geographic Image Collection; pages 12 inset, 26 Corbis; page 12 top SEF/Art Resource, NY; pages 13, 15, 19 The Granger Collection, NY; pages 16–17, 24–25, 40–41, 56 National Geographic Image Collection; page 18 Tom Lovell/National Geographic Image Collection; page 20 The Art Archive/Musée Louvre Paris/Dagli Orti; pages 21, 59 Ancient Art and Architecture; page 22 left Mary Evans Picture Library; page 23 Photodisc/Getty Images; page 27 Bridgeman Art Library; pages 28–29 David Boyer/National Geographic Image Collection; pages 32–33 Michele Burgess/SuperStock; page 34 C.F. Payne/National Geographic Image Collection; page 38 left Photographed at the Egyptian Art Museum/National Geographic Image Collection; page 38 right The Art Archive/Egyptian Museum Cairo/Dagli Orti; page 39 Royalty-Free/Corbis; pages 42–43, 48 The British Museum/Heritage Image Partnership, UK; pages 44–45 Archivo Iconografico, S.A./Corbis; page 46 Bettmann/ Corbis; page 47 University of Pennsylvania Museum of Archaeology and Anthropology; page 51 Photodisc Green/Getty Images; page 58 Christie's Images/Corbis; page 59 Charles and Josette Lenars/Corbis; page 60 Joseph J. Scherschel/Iraq Museum, Baghdad/National Geographic Image Collection; page 61 Giraudon/Art Resource, NY; page 62 Bildarchiv Preussischer Kulturbesitz/Art Resource, NY; page 63 Roger Wood/Corbis; page 64 HIP/Scala/Art Resource, NY.

TEXT CREDITS
"Digging Up the Past" From the book *Talking with Adventurers* edited by Pat Cummings and Linda Cummings, Ph.D. Copyright © 1998 Pat Cummings and Linda Cummings. Published by National Geographic Books. Reprinted by permission.

"The Mummy Hunter and Mr X" from *National Geographic World* (March 2002)

Produced through the worldwide resources of the National Geographic Society, John M. Fahey, Jr., President and Chief Executive Officer; Gilbert M. Grosvenor, Chairman of the Board; Nina D. Hoffman, Executive Vice President and President, Books and Education Publishing Group.

PREPARED BY NATIONAL GEOGRAPHIC SCHOOL PUBLISHING
Ericka Markman, Senior Vice President and President Children's Books and Education Publishing Group; Steve Mico, Senior Vice President, Editorial Director; Marianne Hiland, Executive Editor; Richard Easby, Editorial Manager; Anita Schwartz, Project Editor; Jim Hiscott, Design Manager; Kristin Hanneman, Illustrations Manager; Matt Wascavage, Manager of Publishing Services; Sean Philpotts, Production Manager; Jane Ponton, Production Artist.

MANUFACTURING AND QUALITY CONTROL
Christopher A. Liedel, Chief Financial Officer; Phillip L. Schlosser, Director; Clifton M. Brown III, Manager.

ART DIRECTION Dan Banks, Project Design Company

CONSULTANTS/REVIEWERS
Geoff Emberling, Ph.D., Director, Oriental Institute Museum, University of Chicago; Emily Teeter, Ph.D., Research Associate, Oriental Institute, University of Chicago

BOOK DEVELOPMENT Nieman Inc.

BOOK DESIGN Three Communication Design, LLC

PICTURE EDITING Jill S. Kelly

MAP DEVELOPMENT AND PRODUCTION Mapping Specialists, Ltd.

Published by the National Geographic Society
1145 17th Street, N.W.
Washington, D.C. 20036-4688

ISBN: 978-0-7922-4941-2
ISBN: 0-7922-4941-0

4 5 6 7 8 9 10 19 18 17 16
Printed in the United States of America.

cover: The Sphinx and the pyramid of the pharaoh Khafre at Giza **page 1:** Golden helmet from the Sumerian city of Ur in modern Iraq **page 3** (top): Bronze head of Sargon **page 3** (center right): Egyptian painting of bird hunting in the Nile reeds **page 3** (center left): Archaeologist Juris Zarins directing a dig at Ubar in present-day Oman **page 3** (bottom): Statue of Hammurabi kneeling in prayer

TABLE OF CONTENTS

4 INTRODUCTION

10 Cracking the Code
16 Schools for Scribes
20 A Hero's Quest
24 "A Tooth for a Tooth"
28 The Gifts of the Nile
32 The Pyramid Builders
40 Journey to the Afterlife
46 Riches from the Tombs of Ur
50 Digging Up the Past
54 The Mummy Hunter & Mr. X

58 OVERVIEW
63 Glossary
64 Index

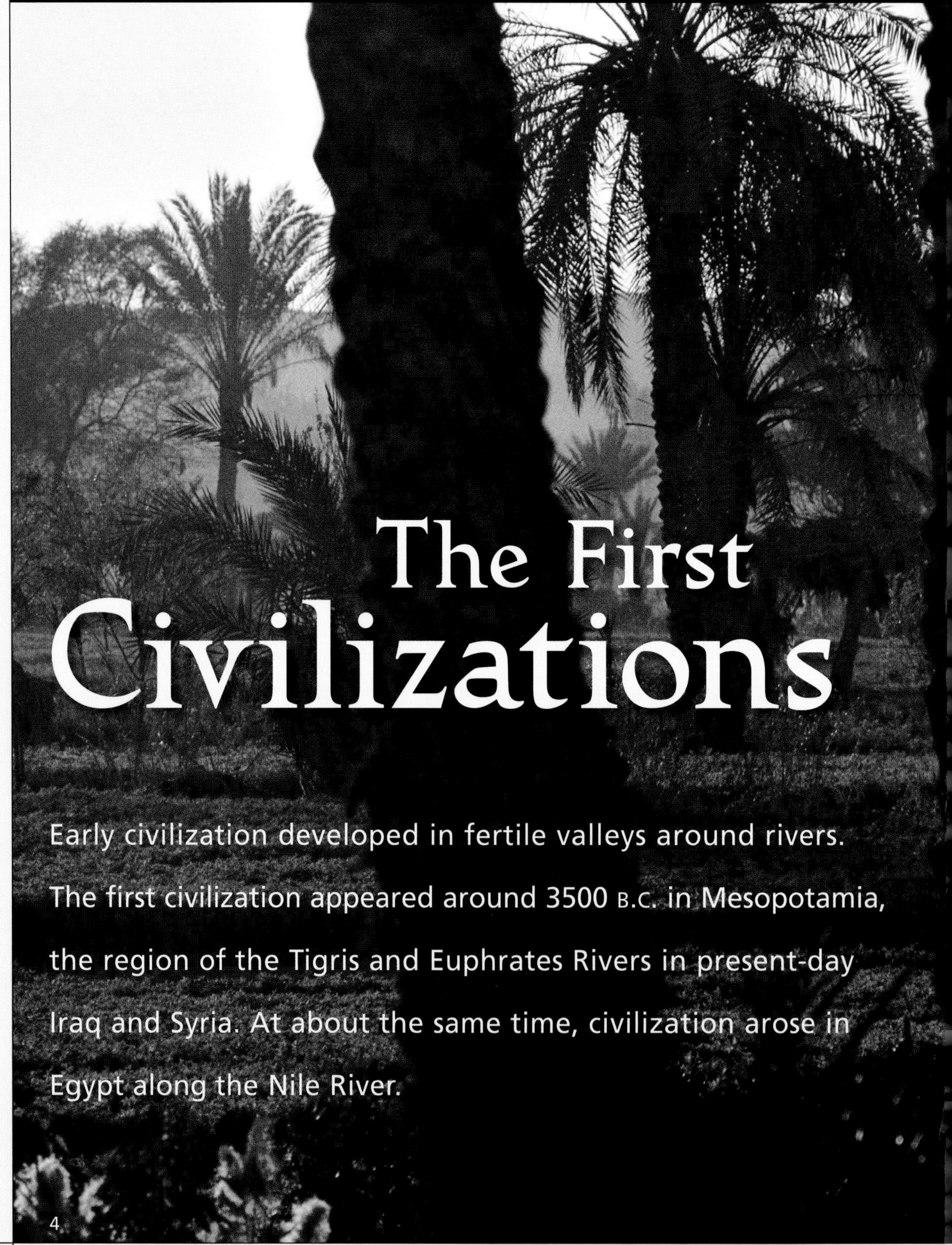

The First Civilizations

Early civilization developed in fertile valleys around rivers. The first civilization appeared around 3500 B.C. in Mesopotamia, the region of the Tigris and Euphrates Rivers in present-day Iraq and Syria. At about the same time, civilization arose in Egypt along the Nile River.

The Step Pyramid, the oldest stone monument in the world, rises behind palm trees lining the Nile River in Egypt.

THE STORY OF THE FIRST CIVILIZATIONS is the story of the first cities. The earliest cities appeared in the basin of the Tigris and Euphrates Rivers. In ancient times, this area was known as Mesopotamia (mes–uh–puh–TAY–mee–uh), meaning "land between the rivers." It was a natural place for people to settle and farm. The soil was fertile, and the rivers provided plentiful water for crops.

Mesopotamia formed part of the **Fertile Crescent**. This region of rich farming and grazing land extended from the Tigris-Euphrates Valley to the coast of the Mediterranean Sea. Many ancient civilizations developed in the Fertile Crescent. A dependable food supply helped the farming villages of ancient Mesopotamia to grow larger. By about 3500 B.C., Mesopotamian peoples had built the world's first cities.

Statue of a Sumerian ruler

Length of Recorded History

3500 B.C. | 3000 B.C. | 2500 B.C.

3500 B.C.
First cities in Sumer

Before 3000 B.C.
Writing invented in Sumer

ANCIENT MESOPOTAMIA AND EGYPT

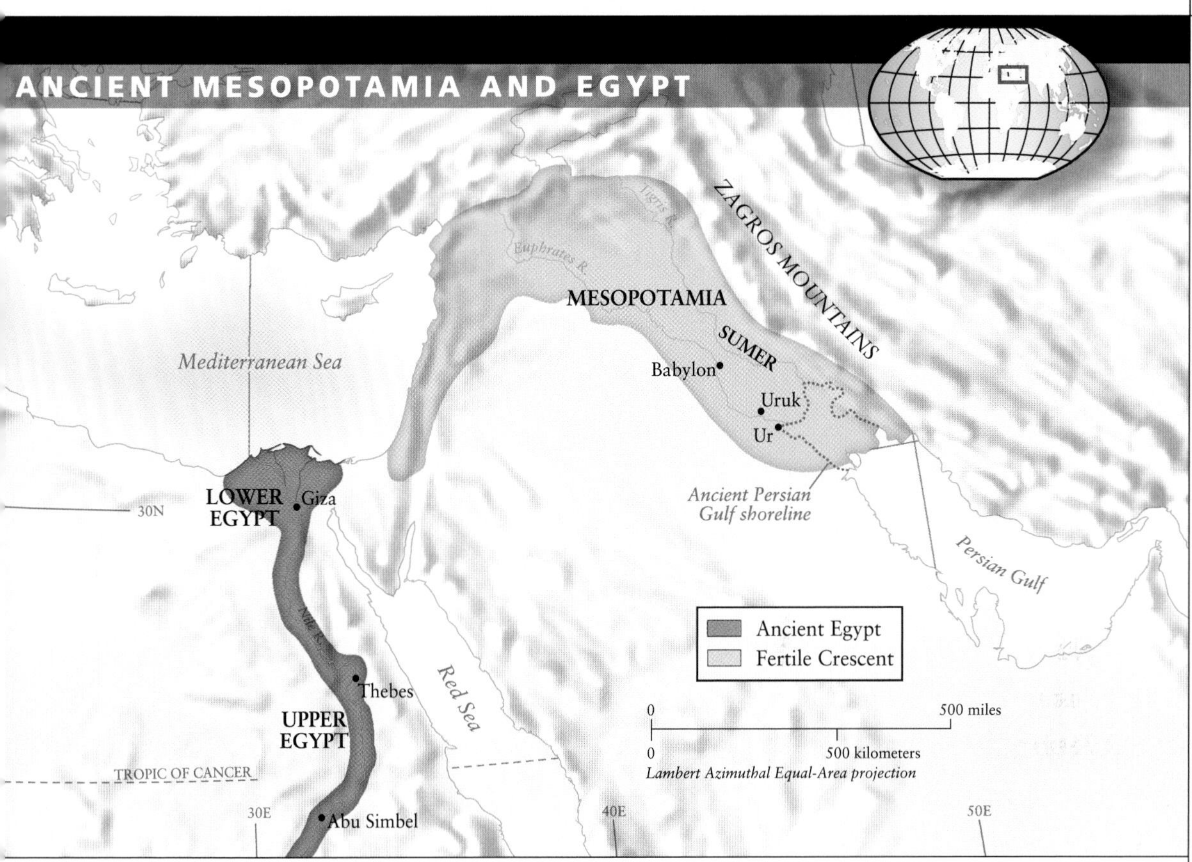

The Sumerians were one of these Mesopotamian peoples. Sumerian cities were something new in human history. They had governments, written records, and laws. Sometime before 3000 B.C., the Sumerians had developed a system of writing to record quantities of goods. They later used writing to record other things, including literature and history.

A new people moved into Sumer about 2000 B.C. Their greatest ruler was Hammurabi (ham–uh–RAH–bee), whose capital city was Babylon on the Euphrates River. To unite his empire, Hammurabi created one of the world's earliest surviving codes of laws around 1750 B.C.

After 1000 B.C.
Egypt in decline

2000 B.C. | 1500 B.C. | 1000 B.C.

At about the same time that cities appeared in Sumer, Egyptian civilization was developing in the valley of the Nile River. As in Mesopotamia, people had settled in the Nile Valley because of its fertile soil and abundant water. The Nile also helped unify Egypt by providing a means of transportation linking the northern and southern parts of the country.

The Egyptians were also unified by their religion and their strong belief in life after death. They are probably best known for the method they developed to preserve dead bodies from decay and for the great pyramid tombs they built to house the bodies of their rulers. Constructing these tombs was a huge project, involving thousands of workers over many years.

About 150 years ago, pioneering **archaeologists,** scientists who study the remains of peoples and cultures of the past, began **excavating** ancient sites in Mesopotamia and Egypt. The vital work of archaeologists in expanding our knowledge of the early civilizations continues today.

The articles in this book describe how the first civilizations developed in ancient Mesopotamia and Egypt and how archaeologists have uncovered them. To help guide your reading, they have been organized around the following three **BIG IDEAS**:

1. Mesopotamia first developed some of the most basic features of civilization, including a system of writing and a code of law.
2. Egyptian civilization was shaped by the Nile River and a concern with the afterlife.
3. Archaeologists study ancient Mesopotamia and Egypt to learn about how civilizations developed.

As you read, keep these ideas in mind. They will help you understand what makes a civilization and how archaeologists work.

BIG IDEA: THE RISE OF CIVILIZATION

1

The world's earliest law codes appeared in ancient Mesopotamia.

BIG IDEA: LIFE AND DEATH IN EGYPT

2

The ancient Egyptians made careful preparations for the afterlife.

BIG IDEA: THE LURE OF THE PAST

3

One of the most important archaeological discoveries of modern times was the royal tombs of the Sumerian city of Ur.

One of the most basic features of any civilization is a system of writing. The work of early archaeologist Henry Rawlinson unlocked the mystery of the writing system the Sumerians had invented to keep their business records.

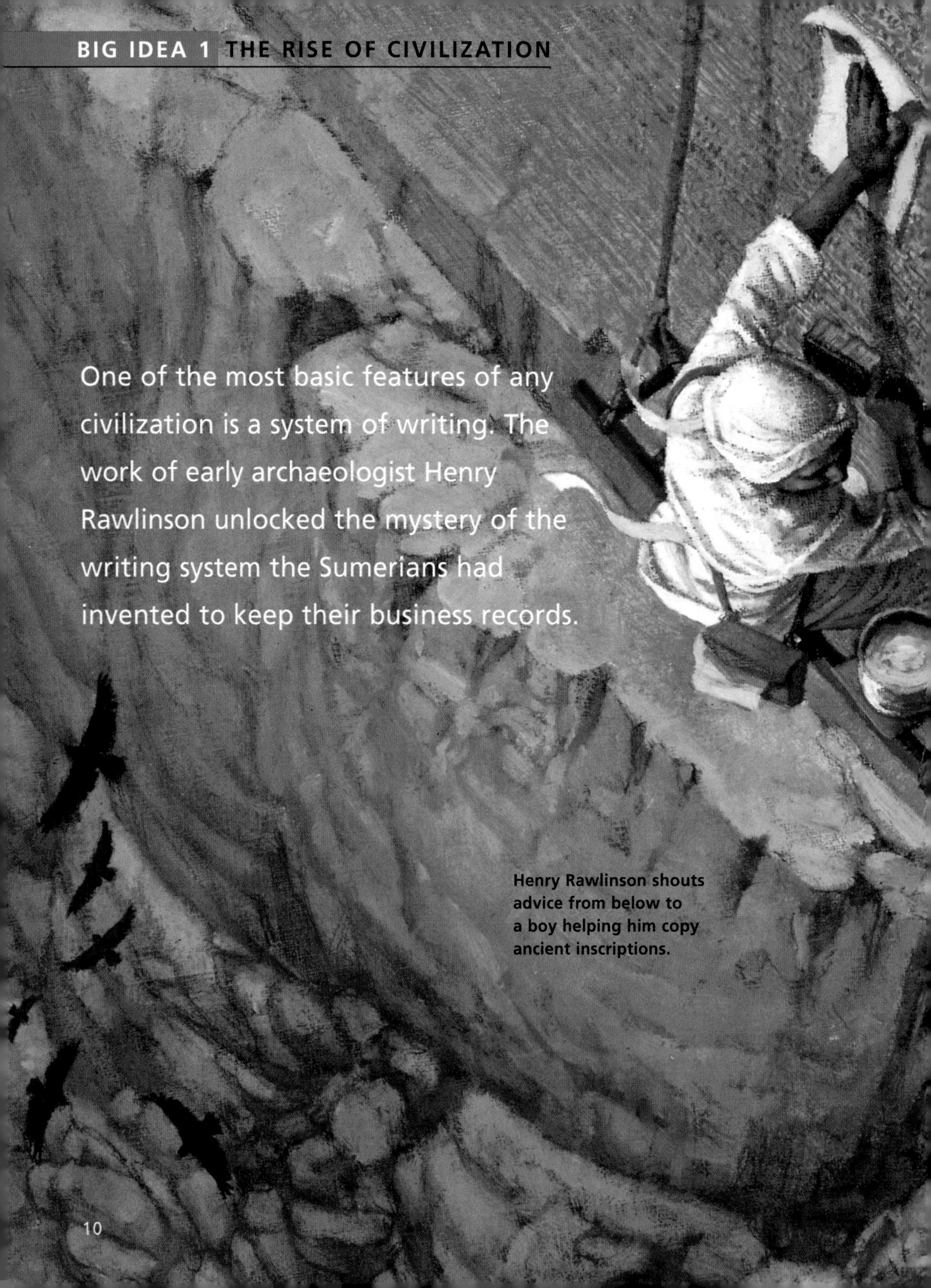

Henry Rawlinson shouts advice from below to a boy helping him copy ancient inscriptions.

Cracking the Code

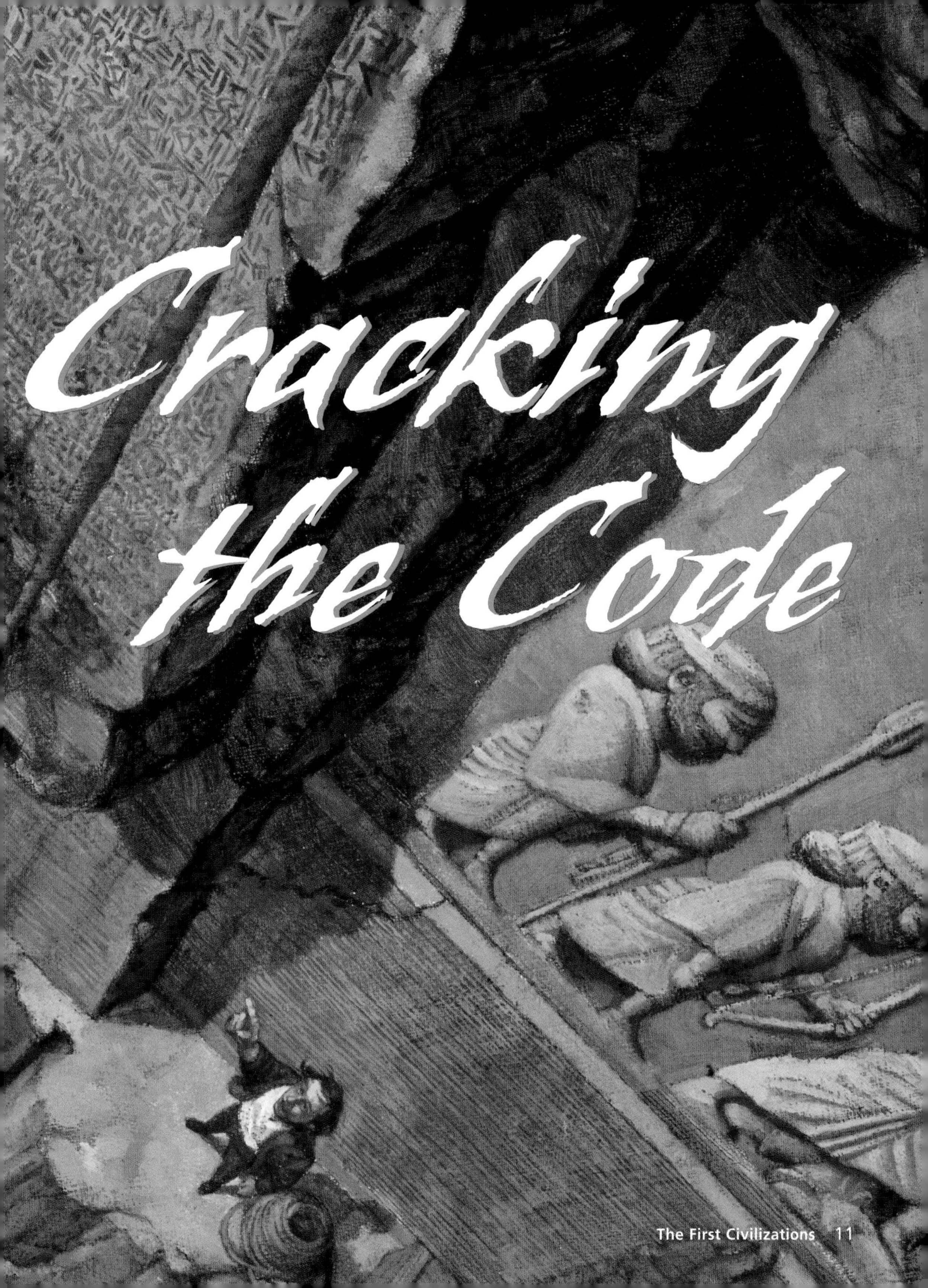

Henry Rawlinson

Figures and inscriptions on the Rock of Behistun

The ancient carvings are high on a cliff beside an old road in what was once the Persian Empire and is now western Iran. Three hundred feet (90 meters) above the ground, people long ago had carefully smoothed and polished an area of the cliff face 18 feet (5.5 meters) across. Then they carved the figures of a Persian king standing in triumph over his defeated enemies. Surrounding these figures on three sides are three different inscriptions.

European visitors to the region had long stopped to gaze at the carvings and wonder what the inscriptions said. One traveler wrote, "What a treasure of information doubtless was there to the happy man who could decipher this writing."

In 1835, a young Englishman named Henry Rawlinson decided to try to **decipher**, or decode, these ancient inscriptions. First, he had to copy them down. Just climbing the steep, slippery cliff, called the Rock of Behistun, was a dangerous adventure. Even today, for an expert climber with modern equipment, it would not be easy. Rawlinson risked his life every time he struggled up the cliff and perched on one of the narrow, rocky ledges to copy the inscriptions.

Rawlinson started with the inscription that was easiest to reach. He copied it by making what he called "squeezes." He pressed damp sheets of paper against the rock face so that they took the impression of the carved letters.

During the years that followed, he returned several times to the Rock of Behistun to copy more of the inscription. In the 1840s, Rawlinson hired a Kurdish boy to copy a part that was very hard to reach. Because the Kurds live in the mountains, Rawlinson knew the boy could handle the height. The young Kurd drove pegs into two slim clefts in the rock face and roped them to a narrow seat on which he sat—300 feet (90 meters) up—to copy the marks.

Reading Cuneiform

During the 12 years that he copied the inscriptions, Rawlinson worked patiently to decipher their meaning. All three were written in the ancient Mesopotamian script known as **cuneiform** (KYOO–nee–uh–form), meaning "wedge-shaped." The writing had hundreds of different characters made up of wedge-shaped marks. When archaeologists began digging up the ruins of Mesopotamian cities, they found thousands of clay tablets covered with cuneiform characters.

Rawlinson discovered that the three different parts of the Behistun inscription were written in three ancient languages of the Middle East. By 1838, Rawlinson had unraveled part of the oldest language.

The inscription told of the military victories of an ancient Persian king, Darius I. The second part was tougher, because it was not related to any language that people still spoke. By 1844, Rawlinson and other scholars deciphered it.

The last part was the hardest of all. It included 500 different cuneiform characters. But it appeared that all three inscriptions told the same story. Rawlinson could use the first two inscriptions to help him decipher the last part. Finally, in 1857, he succeeded in reading it. Rawlinson had cracked the code of cuneiform. In the years to come, other archaeologists would mine the "treasure of information" his work had unlocked.

A cuneiform tablet with wedge-shaped marks

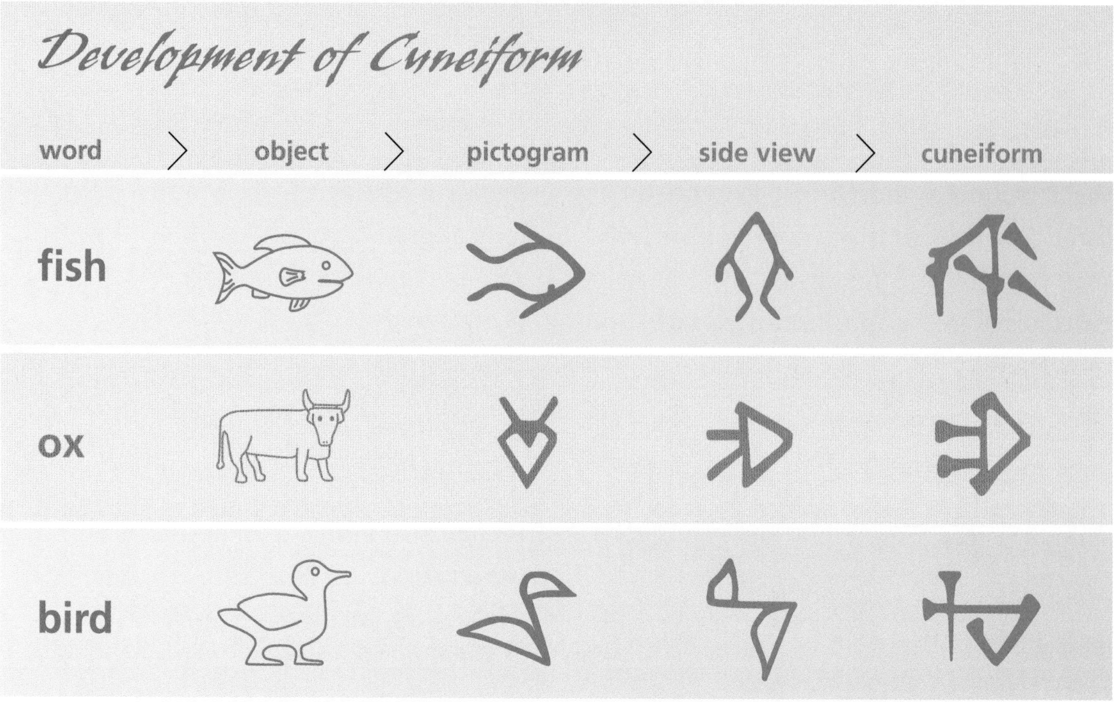

The Beginning of Writing

Cuneiform had actually begun as a method of accounting. The farmers of the ancient Middle East probably first used pebbles to keep track of how much grain or how many animals they owned. Later, they began to mold pieces of clay in different shapes, such as disks or cones. The different shapes stood for different types of goods, such as sheep or sacks of barley.

Using clay shapes or tokens worked for thousands of years, but slowly this system began to change. People started to keep records by pressing a simple picture of a thing into soft clay tablets. A picture used to represent a thing is known as a **pictogram.** As time passed, these pictograms grew even simpler, turning into symbols.

The big step in the development of cuneiform took place when people began using symbols to stand for ideas, not just things. For example, the symbol for the idea "to eat" combined the symbol for "mouth" with the symbol for "food." By about 3200 B.C., the Sumerians had developed simple pictograms into a writing system with hundreds of characters.

Cuneiform was a system of writing, not a spoken language, like English, Spanish, or French. Although these three languages are different, they are all written with the same alphabet.

The Rosetta Stone

In 1799, near the small Egyptian town of Rosetta, a French soldier discovered a large stone slate covered with strange markings. Like the Behistun inscriptions, the Rosetta Stone contained the same message written in three different scripts.

The first was the picture writing known as **hieroglyphs** (HI–uhr–uh–glihfs), from Greek words meaning "sacred carving." Ancient Egyptians used hieroglyphs for important inscriptions and documents. The second script was a rounded form used for more ordinary writing. The third script was ancient Greek.

A Frenchman named Jean-François Champollion spent years studying the Rosetta Stone. He used his knowledge of Greek to figure out what the two other types of writing meant. In 1822, he finally deciphered the inscriptions. Archaeologists were now able to read ancient Egyptian writings. The Rosetta Stone was the key to understanding the civilization of ancient Egypt.

In the same way, the Sumerians and later peoples used the cuneiform writing system to write their own languages. Cuneiform became the most widely used writing system of the ancient Middle East. People used it to record tax payments, wages, contracts, and laws. They wrote prayers and recorded tales in cuneiform. Most importantly, they used it to write down their history.

▸ *For more information about the Sumerians, see pages 59–60.*

WHY IT MATTERS TODAY

Once archaeologists cracked the code of cuneiform, they unlocked a treasure of information about life in one of the world's earliest civilizations. From ancient times until today, the written word tells the story of civilization.

SCHOOLS FOR SCRIBES

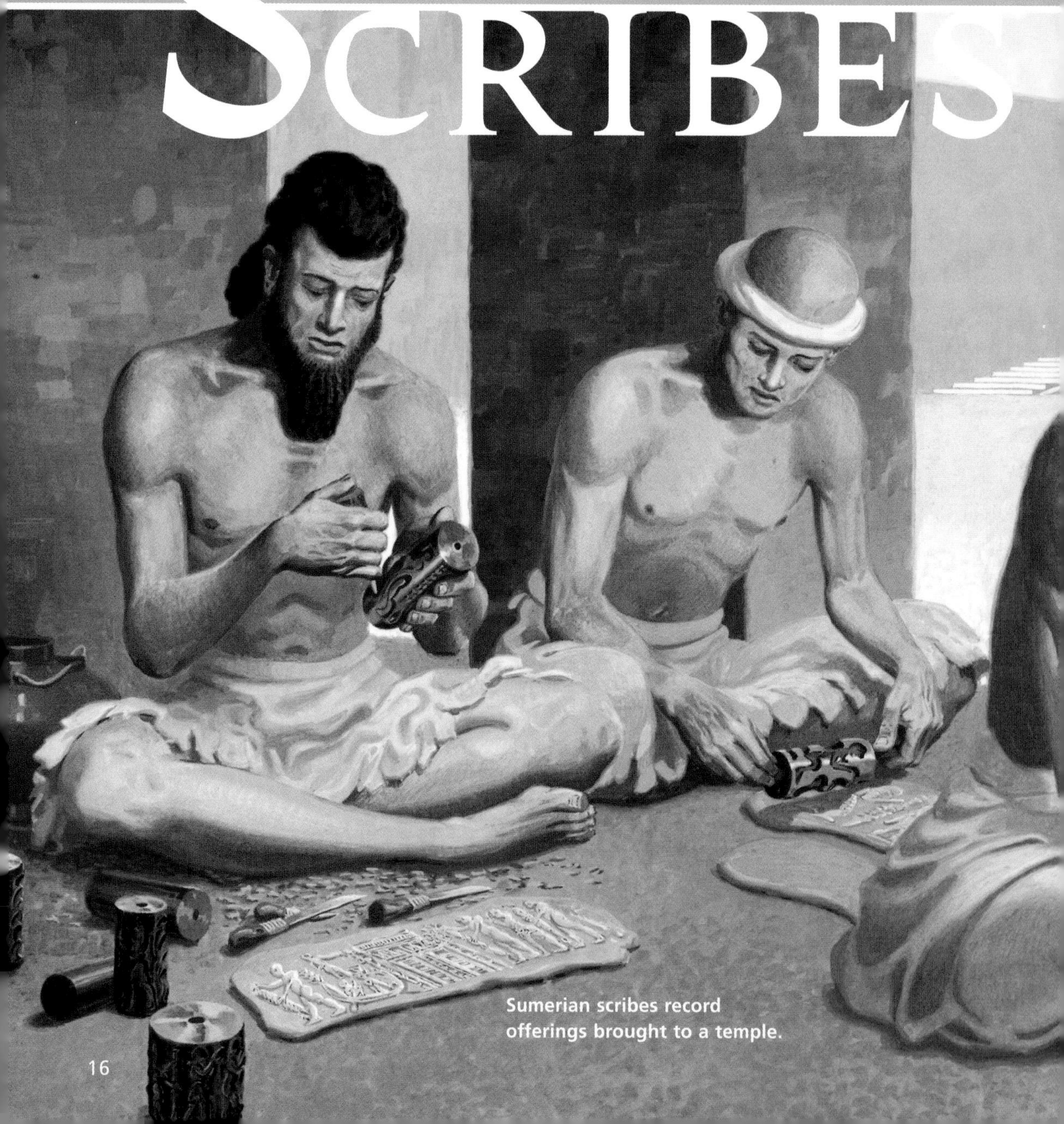

Sumerian scribes record offerings brought to a temple.

Written records were essential to Mesopotamian civilization. The people who kept these records received special training that began when they were children.

Learning to write in ancient Sumer was much harder than just knowing your ABCs. Cuneiform writing included hundreds of different symbols that combined to form words. Few people learned to read and write this complex script. Those that did, called **scribes**, carried out very important work for Sumerian society.

The cities of Sumer employed many different types of scribes. Some scribes worked for the king. Others kept temple records. As with any kind of learning, some people became better scribes than others. One Sumerian proverb says that the best scribes could take notes while listening to a speaker. Some scribes, on the other hand, could not even spell properly.

As the cities of Sumer grew, they needed more and more scribes to keep their records. The first schools in history were created in Sumer to teach boys how to be scribes. Because scribes used a wedge-shaped instrument called a **stylus** to press cuneiform signs into wet clay tablets, the Sumerians called their schools "**tablet houses.**"

School Days in Sumer

The head teacher who ran each tablet house was the "school father." A student was called a "school son." Another teacher, known as "big brother," assisted the school father. This assistant's duties included checking the tablets that the students copied for practice. Archaeologists have found many of these practice tablets in the ruins of Sumerian cities. The cuneiform writing on them ranges from the crude work of beginners to the careful script of advanced students.

Most of the students at the tablet houses came from wealthy families. They spent 12 years studying nearly all day. First, the students learned how to write signs for basic sounds and simple words. Later, they learned signs for special groups of words, such as legal and government terms, geographic terms, parts of the body, food, and drink. They learned how to write letters and inscriptions for monuments. They also learned mathematics and music.

▶ *For more information about Sumerian civilization, see pages 59–60.*

WHY IT MATTERS TODAY

To teach its scribes, Mesopotamia created the first organized system of education in human history. All the familiar elements of modern schools, including teachers, textbooks, and a curriculum, began in ancient Sumer.

What about the Girls?

No girls attended the Sumerian tablet houses, but some were trained at home. Tutors taught them to be scribes. When their education was complete, they became priestesses of the Mesopotamian sun god Shamash (SHAH–mahsh) and especially of his goddess wife Aya. More than 140 of these female scribes lived at Aya's temple in the city of Sippar. Like male scribes, they had endured years of hard training and came from wealthy families.

These priestesses bought and sold land and slaves. They kept the temple records, noting what money people gave for offerings and what the temple spent. They were important members of the community. A few of the priestesses were married, but none were allowed to have children. Much of what we know about the lives of Sumerian women comes from records they left behind.

A statue of Gilgamesh holding a lion cub

The peoples of ancient Mesopotamia created the world's first great work of literature, the *Epic of Gilgamesh*. It tells of a king's desperate search for the secret of eternal life.

A Hero's Quest

"Because of my brother I am afraid of death, because of my brother I stray through the wilderness and cannot rest."

— *EPIC OF GILGAMESH*

Utnapishtim in his enchanted garden (left); The demon Humbaba (below)

The ancient Sumerians told many tales of their heroes Gilgamesh and Enkidu (en–KI–doo). In today's terms, they might be called superheros. Their story deals with the meaning of life and death. We had better start at the beginning.

In this tale, Gilgamesh, who is part god and part man, rules the Sumerian city of Uruk. The people of Uruk fear him and pray to the gods for protection from their king. So the gods create Enkidu, a wild man who is stronger than any animal. Enkidu challenges Gilgamesh to a fight, but he has to admit Gilgamesh is stronger. From then on, the two heroes are best friends.

A giant named Humbaba lives far up the Euphrates River, in a sacred forest where he guards the trees for the gods. The heroes journey to the forest. There they fight Humbaba and cut off his head. The death of Humbaba enrages the gods. They send a horrible monster, the Bull of Heaven, to attack Uruk. Gilgamesh and Enkidu fight and kill the Bull of Heaven as well.

Now the gods are even angrier. They curse Enkidu as a punishment. Gilgamesh watches his friend sicken and die. Grief-stricken, Gilgamesh is also afraid because he knows that someday, like Enkidu, he will die too. He believes the only way he can live with his grief and fear is to find the secret of eternal life.

The Secret of Eternal Life

Gilgamesh begins his quest. He knows he needs to find Utnapishtim (oot–nah–PEESH–teem), an old man who had survived a great flood long ago. Now Utnapishtim lives on an enchanted island far away. When Gilgamesh finally reaches the island, he begs the old man for the secret of eternal life. Utnapishtim first tells him the story of the flood.

Long ago, the old man tells Gilgamesh, the gods had decided to create a huge flood to wipe out all living things. One god, however, warned Utnapishtim of the coming danger. The old man built a huge ship to save himself, his family, and some of every living thing. Then the flood came. "The god of the storm turned daylight to darkness, when he smashed the land like a cup." For six days and seven nights, the storm raged. On the seventh day, the rain stopped. Utnapishtim looked out from his boat. Water stretched everywhere, like a flat roof. All living things, except those on the boat, died.

Gilgamesh again pleads with Utnapishtim to give him the secret of eternal life. Out of pity, the old man tells him of a magic plant that grows at the bottom of the sea. One prick of the plant's thorns will restore a person's youth. Gilgamesh ties stones to his feet and dives to the bottom of the sea, where he finds the magic plant.

The hero starts his long journey back to Uruk. One night, while Gilgamesh sleeps, a snake finds the plant and eats it. When the hero realizes he has lost the secret of eternal youth and is fated to die, he weeps. Gilgamesh knows that he has no choice but to return to Uruk and face death. When the hero reaches home, he finds some peace in the knowledge that his city is strong and will endure.

▶ *For more information about ancient Mesopotamia, see pages 59–60.*

WHY IT MATTERS TODAY

Literature is an important aspect of civilization. In their literature, civilizations express their values and ideals. The world's first great work of literature, the *Epic of Gilgamesh*, is a passionate protest against death.

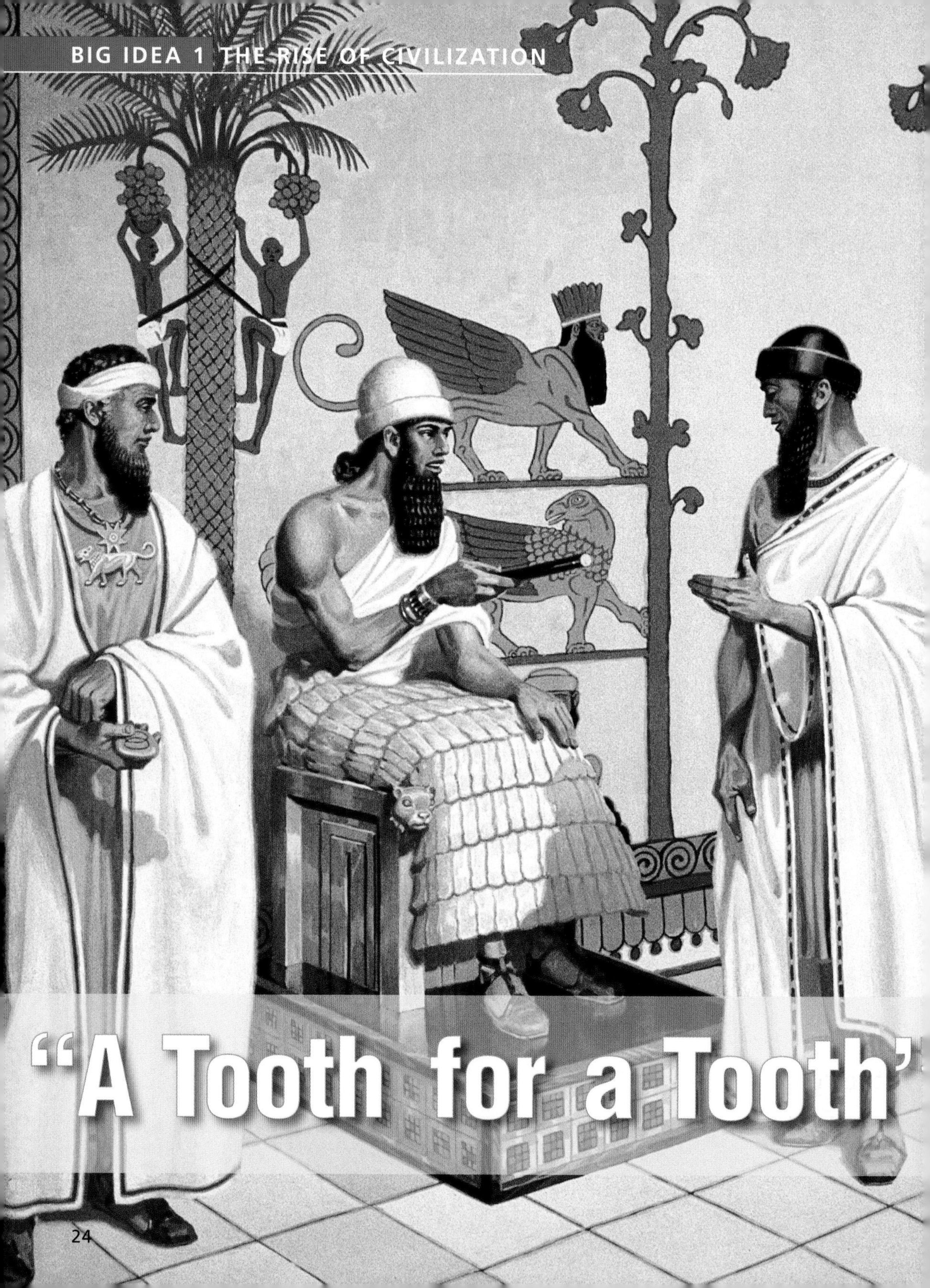

"A Tooth for a Tooth"

Hammurabi meets with his advisers.

Laws are an essential part of any civilization. Around 1750 B.C., the ruler of ancient Mesopotamia wrote down on a stone pillar all the laws that the people throughout his empire had to obey.

The larger and more complex a society becomes, the more its people need laws to keep their community running smoothly and safely. The ancient Mesopotamian king Hammurabi ruled one of the world's first empires. To improve the well-being of his people and "to keep the strong from harming the weak," he created a code of 282 laws. We know about Hammurabi's Code because he carved many of his laws on a pillar of hard black stone 8 feet (2.5 meters) high. It was found by a French archaeologist in 1901.

Hammurabi's Code is the most complete legal system that has survived from ancient Mesopotamia. How did his laws work? In general, Hammurabi made the punishment match the crime. For example, a man who knocked out another person's teeth should have his own tooth knocked out.

Hammurabi's Code dealt harshly with crime. Breaking into someone's house, for instance, was punishable by death. Men who struck their fathers had their hands cut off. The Code of Hammurabi does not mention prison as a punishment for crime.

Many of Hammurabi's 282 laws covered noncriminal matters, such as marriages and business contracts. Today, these are called **civil laws,** which deal with people's rights. Some of Hammurabi's civil laws explained the conditions under which a married couple could separate.

Some of his laws dealt with what we call consumer protection today. For example, if an animal doctor performed

Hammurabi had his laws carved onto this stone pillar, or *stele.* The scene at the top shows Hammurabi (standing) receiving the laws from the sun god Shamash.

ACROSS CULTURES

THE TEN COMMANDMENTS

The most famous law code in Western civilization is the Ten Commandments. According to the Bible, it was originally written on stone like Hammurabi's Code. But in other important ways, the two law codes are different.

The Jewish leader Moses with the stone tablets on which the Ten Commandments were written

Hammurabi's Code is a collection of decisions that the king made in response to specific cases. For example, Hammurabi says that if someone steals property from a burning house while helping to put out the fire, the thief shall be burned to death. By contrast, the Ten Commandments are more general. For example, one says, "Thou shalt not steal." It does not describe a specific type of theft or indicate a punishment.

Hammurabi's Code provides different rulings depending on the social class of the people involved in the case. For example, if a free man strikes another free man, he must pay a fine. If a slave strikes a free man, the slave's ear must be cut off. The Ten Commandments makes no such distinctions. All of its laws apply equally to everyone.

an operation on an ox and killed it, he had to pay the owner a fourth of its value. If a shipbuilder's boat leaked, he had to take it apart and make it waterproof at his own expense.

For more information about Hammurabi, see page 60.

WHY IT MATTERS TODAY

The Code of Hammurabi is the most important law code to survive from ancient Mesopotamia. Its laws provide a detailed picture of Mesopotamian civilization and mark the beginning of formal legal systems in human society.

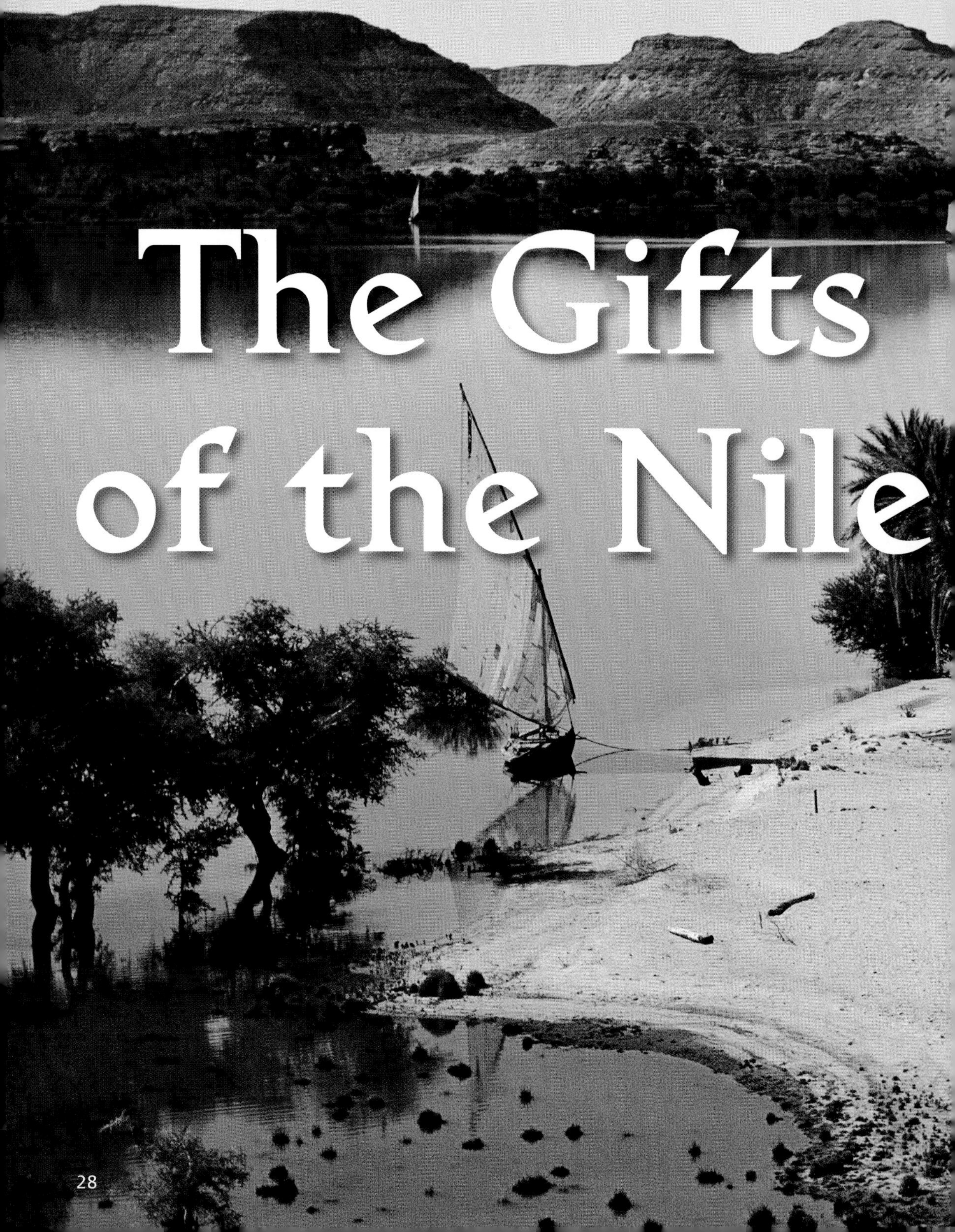

The Gifts of the Nile

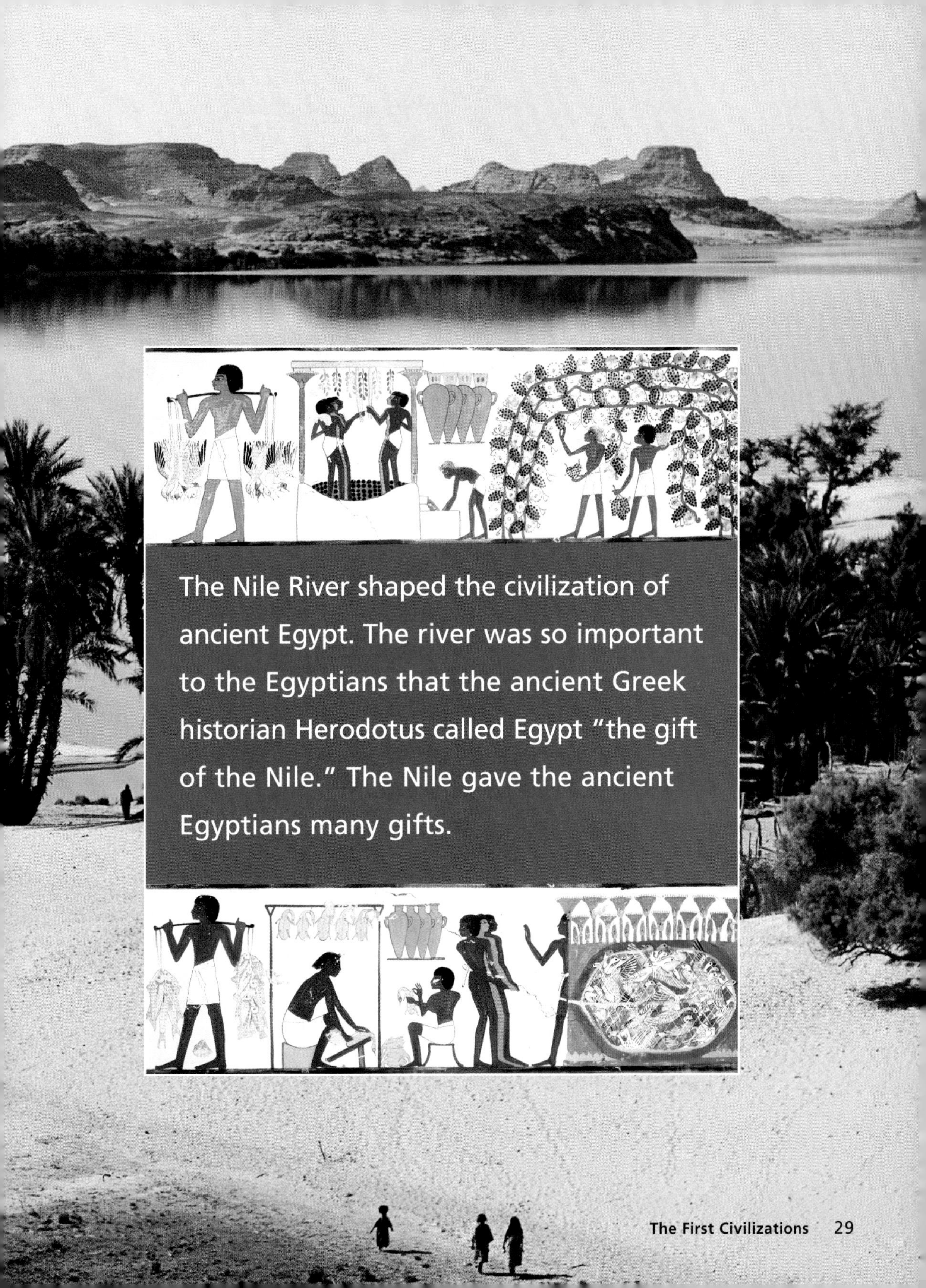

The Nile River shaped the civilization of ancient Egypt. The river was so important to the Egyptians that the ancient Greek historian Herodotus called Egypt "the gift of the Nile." The Nile gave the ancient Egyptians many gifts.

Ancient Egyptians hunting birds near the Nile

People of the River

The Nile's most important gift to the Egyptians was food. Egypt does not get enough rainfall to farm. Yet the Nile Valley became one of the greatest food-producing regions of the ancient world. This was possible because each summer, heavy rains in the highlands of Africa, far to the south, caused the Nile to overflow its banks and spread over the surrounding countryside. This annual flooding left behind a fertile layer of mud called **silt** on Egypt's fields, renewing the soil. Because of the rich, dark color of the silt, the Egyptians called their country Kemet, "the black land."

At its mouth, the Nile fans out into a **delta,** forming a vast triangle of marshland. The Nile Delta was the home of millions of wild birds, another source of food. More important, these marshes were full of tall reeds called **papyrus** (puh–PI–ruhs). In ancient times, the Egyptians used the soft material inside the stems of these reeds to make a type of paper also called papyrus. (Papyrus is the source of our word *paper.*) The Egyptians used papyrus for all kinds of writing, from legal documents to hymns.

The Nile River also helped to unify and organize Egyptian society.

"Hail to you, O Nile!
Sprung from Earth,
Come to nourish Egypt!
Food provider, bounty maker, Who creates all that is good."

—Egyptian hymn to the Nile

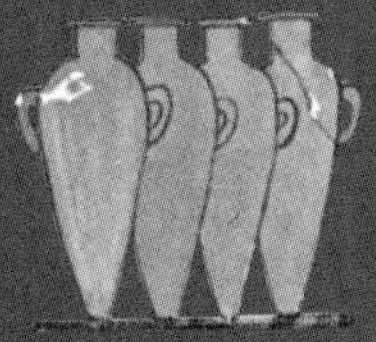

Egyptian farmers still needed water after the Nile flood receded each year. So the ancient Egyptians dug canals to bring river water to their fields. Digging these canals and keeping them working forced the ancient Egyptians to develop the beginnings of government. A complex project such as building a canal required the organization of groups of laborers. Some government officials held the title "Overseer of the Canal," which shows how important this work was in ancient Egypt.

An ancient Egyptian poem says, "The waters flow north, the wind blows south, and each man meets his fate."

These lines reveal another of the Nile's gifts to ancient Egypt—transportation and trade. The river flows north, so northbound ships simply traveled with the current. The prevailing winds blow from north to south, so southbound boats would hoist a wide sail to travel upstream. In this way, the Nile became Egypt's great highway. It was the fastest way to travel through the country. Grain and other goods traveled up and down the river. Egypt's rulers depended on the river to transport the huge stones that were used to build their great tombs and temples.

The Nile was so important to the ancient Egyptians that they worshipped the river as a god, Osiris (oh–SI–rihs). Osiris died and was reborn, like the Nile, whose waters brought new life to Egypt each year.

▶ *For more information about ancient Egypt, see pages 61–62.*

WHY IT MATTERS TODAY

From ancient times to the present, the life of Egypt has depended on the Nile. In modern times, the Egyptian government built the Aswan High Dam to control the Nile's flooding and produce electric power. So today the Nile brings another gift to Egypt—energy.

THE PYRAMID BUILDERS

The most visible sign of the greatness of ancient Egyptian civilization is the pyramids. Built as a combination of temple and tomb for Egyptian rulers, these colossal monuments have drawn visitors to Egypt for 4,500 years.

A line of camels travels past the massive pyramids of Giza. Nearby are remains of the village that housed the workers who toiled on the project.

For more than 4,500 years, the Great Pyramid of Giza has stood in the Egyptian desert. For most of that time, no taller structure existed on Earth. It contains more than two million blocks of stone. Most of the blocks weigh about 5,000 pounds (2,300 kilograms) each—about as much as a large pickup truck. Some larger blocks weigh 100,000 pounds (45,000 kilograms) each—about as much as a small tugboat.

The workers who built this mountain of stone had simple tools. They used stone picks and copper chisels to cut the blocks and trim them so that they fit snugly together.

Other laborers first dragged the huge blocks up ramps stretching from the sides of the partly completed pyramid and then fitted the stones into place. Who were these workers? People used to believe they were slaves. Archaeologists today have uncovered a different view of the pyramid builders.

How Did They Live?

Egypt's ruler, the **pharaoh** Khufu, started planning the Great Pyramid as soon as he came to the throne.

Workers bring a boatload of stone to be used in building the pyramid rising in the distance.

About 4,000 people worked year-round for 20 years or more to create Khufu's Great Pyramid. They included engineers, artists, stonecutters, and laborers. These full-time pyramid builders may have been helped by up to 20,000 part-time workers who built ramps, made tools, and mixed mortar. These workers also would have provided support services, such as supplying food and clothing.

In order to pile up two million stone blocks in 20 years' time, pharaoh's workers had to set one in place every few minutes. They needed an organized village to support this fast pace of work.

During the many years it took to build a pyramid, a town arose nearby to house the full-time workers and their families. Part-time workers probably lived in temporary camps outside this town. At the Giza pyramid site, archaeologists have uncovered a complete walled village, with the remains of neat rows of mud-brick houses. Well-designed buildings, including bakeries and workshops, lined the paved streets. The village had a drainage system to carry off waste.

At the Giza village, we know the

A restoration worker cuts stone for the Giza pyramids.

At the Giza village, we know the workers and their families raised ducks, sheep, pigs, and cows. The writing, pottery, clothing, tools, children's toys, and garbage found there suggest that the laborers led ordinary lives when they were not at work on the Great Pyramid.

The Egyptians had a system of dividing workers into groups and then into smaller teams, each with its own leader. Each team tackled a different part of the project, such as raising walls or building interior rooms. In this way, the large number of workers was more manageable. The pyramid builders took pride in their work. Some of the building stones still show team autographs, such as "Friends of Khufu" or "Boat Gang." These teams may have competed with each other to see who could work the fastest.

On average, the men of the Giza village lived 40 to 45 years, while women lived 30 to 35 years. When they died, villagers were buried in a graveyard that held various kinds of monuments. Their small tombs were made of mud and stone. Some graves were carved into rocky cliffs and decorated with hieroglyphs. Others were just small

Archaeologist Momadouh Taha examines a tomb in the builders' cemetery. This tomb belonged to a construction overseer.

mounds of dirt. Pyramid builders could not afford to have their bodies preserved as **mummies** or to be buried in elaborate tombs. Still, most were buried with objects such as knives and jewelry that they wanted in the afterlife.

Experts who study the dig at Giza have learned about the health of the villagers by studying their skeletons. Almost all of the men and women had arthritis. This disease of the joints slowly makes it hard for people to walk and lift things. There were doctors at Giza. One worker's skeleton shows that a doctor amputated his injured arm skillfully enough to allow it to heal well.

These statues all portray a carpenter who oversaw the making of tools and boats at Giza.

Why Did They Do It?

The part-time pyramid builders were Egyptian farmers. They may have worked three or four months, perhaps during the times that the Nile flooded the lowlands, and their farms were unworkable. The full-time workers were not slaves. They may have been required by the government to work on the pyramids, something like being drafted to serve in the army. Or they may have been volunteers willing to help on this great project.

The pyramid builders must have felt a sense of pride. They worked to assure everlasting life for their pharaoh, and, through the ruler, for themselves and for Egypt as well. These laborers used their own strength and simple technology to complete one of history's most impressive and long-lasting building projects.

▶ *For more information about ancient Egypt, see pages 61–62.*

WHY IT MATTERS TODAY

The great pyramids of Egypt are among the world's oldest, largest, and most famous monuments. In recent years, archaeologists have learned much about the lives of the workers who built the pyramids.

MAKING PHAROAH LOOK GOOD

MAKE PHARAOH VERY LARGE. Ramses placed dozens of colossal statues of himself throughout Egypt. These at the temple of Abu Simbel are 60 feet (18 meters) tall.

The art of a civilization provides important clues about its values. The artists of ancient Egypt spent much of their time picturing pharaoh. Most of this art presents pharaoh as a mighty, godlike figure. There were different ways of making pharaoh look good.

MAKE PHARAOH LOOK TOUGH.
Ramses II was one of ancient Egypt's greatest empire-builders. This carved panel shows him in battle grabbing some of his enemies by the hair.

PICTURE PHARAOH AS A MAN—EVEN IF SHE IS A WOMAN.
Statues of Hatshepsut, one of Egypt's few female rulers, show her as a man. Here she wears the ceremonial false beard of a pharaoh.

Journey to

The ancient Egyptians believed that death was only the beginning of happiness in the afterlife. To help the souls of the dead to reach this goal safely, the living made careful preparations.

These figures, known as *ushabtis,* were placed in tombs by the ancient Egyptians to serve the soul of the dead person.

the Afterlife

Pharaoh was setting out on his last, but most important, journey—to the world of the dead. His soul would travel in a boat like the one in which the sun god Ra traveled through the underworld each night. Like the sun god, pharaoh would face dangers on his journey. The greatest threat was a huge serpent whose terrifying roars echoed through the darkness. But when these dangers were passed, he would be reborn like the sun and live forever.

Death and Judgment

Egyptians believed that people's souls lived on in the peaceful world of the dead. They called this land the "Beautiful West," because it was located where the sun set. To reach the Beautiful West, pharaoh's soul must first make a dangerous journey through the underworld where monsters might attack it. To protect souls from danger, Egyptians placed in tombs the *Book of the Dead,* a collection of prayers and magic spells.

At the end of its journey through the underworld, pharaoh's soul reached the Hall of the Two Truths, where it faced judgment. Pharaoh's heart was weighed on a scale against a feather that stood for truth. If his heart, weighed down by sins, was heavier than this feather, pharaoh's soul would be devoured by a terrible monster with the head of a crocodile. If the scales balanced, his soul would be led before the god Osiris and accepted into the afterlife to live on forever.

The ancient Egyptians believed that the god Osiris ruled the dead. The sun god Ra first made Osiris and his wife Isis (I–sihs) king and queen of Egypt. The Egyptians loved Osiris for his kindness and wisdom, but his brother Seh became jealous and killed him. Seh cut his brother's body into many pieces and scattered them across Egypt. The grieving Isis put Osiris's body back together. She used magic, but could not bring him fully back to life. Since the spirit of Osiris lived on, Ra made him king of the dead.

"I have not done evil. . . .
I have not inflicted pain.
I have not caused
anyone to go hungry.
I have not made any
man to weep. . . .
I am pure. I am pure.
I am pure."

—Book of the Dead

The heart of the dead person is weighed against the feather of Truth (left). He is then escorted to Osiris, the chief god of the afterlife, who is seated in a shrine (right).

Preparing for Death

The well-being of Egypt depended on pharaoh surviving in the afterlife. So preparations for his death began years before he died. Work on a pharaoh's tomb often started as soon as he came to power. To house their tombs, some pharaohs built huge pyramids. Others cut great temples into the cliffs of the Valley of the Kings. All these tombs had hidden entrances to stop thieves who might try to steal the treasures buried with the pharaohs.

Tombs contained several rooms. Their walls were painted with scenes of the king being judged by the gods and with religious texts to protect him in the afterlife. The rooms were also filled with everything the pharaoh could want or need in the afterlife. Egyptians thought that life in the Beautiful West would be just like life in this world. So they buried food, clothes, jewelry, weapons, furniture, and many other things with pharaoh.

The most important preparations for the afterlife happened after pharaoh died. In order to give his soul a place to live, pharaoh's body must not be allowed to rot. In ancient Egypt, a body was preserved by being made into a mummy.

The **embalmers** who made mummies were a special group of workers who lived apart from other Egyptians. To make a mummy, these workers first removed the dead person's brain by sticking a sharp tool up through the nose. The Egyptians threw the brains away because they did not value them.

An Egyptian embalmer wears the mask of Anubis, the jackal-headed god who was the guardian of the dead.

They believed the heart was the center of thought and feeling. Next, they make a cut in the belly and pulled out the liver, lungs, stomach, and intestines. These organs were preserved in special jars. The embalmers rinsed the inside of the body with wine and filled it with herbs and spices.

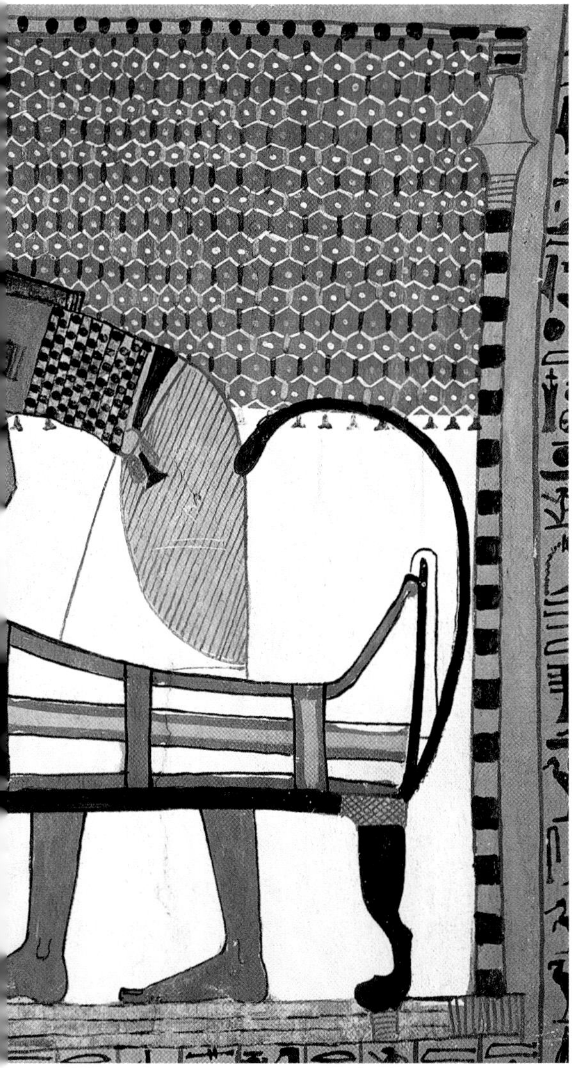

Then they covered the body with a special salt and left it to dry for at least 40 days. When the body was completely dry, the embalmers sewed it back up and anointed it with scented oils. Finally, they wrapped the body in many layers of linen, covered the face with a mask, and placed the completed mummy inside a painted coffin.

Pharaoh was given a grand funeral, celebrating his entrance into the afterlife. He was brought to his tomb, where priests performed a ritual to open his mouth, giving him the breath of eternal life. When the tomb was sealed, pharaoh could begin his journey. The priests would come back often to offer prayers and food for the pharaoh.

For more information about ancient Egypt, see pages 61–62.

WHY IT MATTERS TODAY

Because of their concern with the afterlife, the ancient Egyptians preserved the bodies of their dead with great care and gave them elaborate burials. Much of what we know about ancient Egypt today is based on examining Egyptian tombs and their contents.

Riches
from the Tombs of Ur

Modern archaeology dates from the late 1800s, when systematic excavation of ancient sites—as opposed to treasure hunting—really began. One of the first modern archaeologists was Leonard Woolley.

Leonard Woolley brushes off a clay tablet found at Ur, located in present-day Iraq.

"I found the intact tomb," reported the telegram to the British Museum, "stone built and vaulted with bricks, of Queen Puabi adorned with a dress in which gems, flower crown, and animal figures are woven. Tomb magnificent with jewels and golden cups." That is what the telegram said, except it was written in Latin! British archaeologist Leonard Woolley wanted to keep his great discovery secret from possible rivals or even grave robbers.

Golden headdress from the tomb of Queen Puabi

Just as remarkable as the art and jewelry, however, were the **buried bodies** of her attendants.

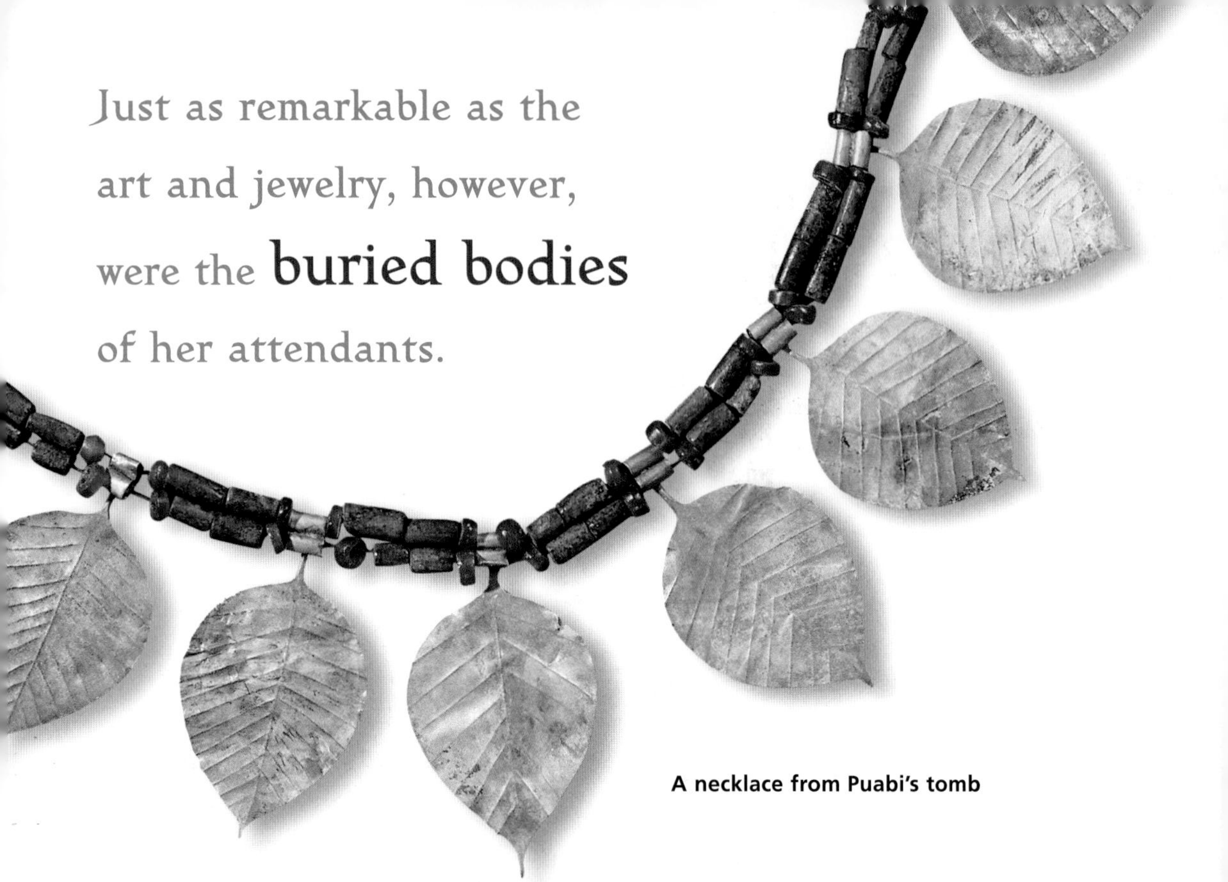

A necklace from Puabi's tomb

The year was 1928. Woolley had already been working for six years to excavate ancient burials at Ur, one of the most important Sumerian cities.

Woolley and his **expedition** uncovered about 1,850 burials in all. He classified 16 of these as "royal" tombs because of the way they were built and the valuable objects they contained. The royal tombs were large underground structures with several rooms. But the tombs also held a grim secret. Buried with a great person were the bodies of servants who had been killed to attend their royal masters in the afterlife.

Over the centuries, looters had broken into most of these royal tombs and carried away unknown treasures. But Woolley found a royal tomb that the grave robbers had missed. In it, a queen's skeleton lay on a wooden platform. She wore a cape made from strings of semiprecious stone beads. She had rings on all her fingers, necklaces, and large gold earrings. On her head, was an elaborate headdress of thousands of beads and gold ribbons, leaves, and flowers. A royal seal, or stamp, with the name Puabi (poo–AH–bee) on it told Woolley whose tomb he had discovered.

Servants for the Afterlife

Just as remarkable as the art and jewelry, however, were the buried bodies of her attendants. In the burial chamber, Woolley found five armed guards, four servants accompanying a wooden sled drawn by a pair of oxen, and more than a dozen other attendants.

It seems they had been celebrating a great feast just before being buried together. One woman still had her hands in position to play a harp. How did they die? No one knows for sure. They seem to have died peacefully. Did they poison themselves willingly in order to continue to serve their queen after death?

Nearby, Woolley found the tomb of a king. It too held sleds, oxen, musical instruments, game boards, cosmetic containers, sculptures, and other wonderful works of art. It also contained the bodies of 63 of his servants. Some had been buried in bright red robes and were heavily adorned with jewelry. Although this tomb had survived, the king's body was missing.

For more information about ancient Sumerian civilization, see pages 59–60.

WHY IT MATTERS TODAY

The royal tombs of Ur were one of the most remarkable archaeological discoveries of the 20th century. The discovery increased knowledge of the richness of Sumerian civilization. Today, you can see the treasures from Ur in museums in Philadelphia, London, and Baghdad.

A golden decoration on a stringed instrument from Puabi's tomb

Digging Up the Past

An Interview with Dr. Juris Zarins

Modern technology has made great changes in archaeology today, and the lone archaeologist has been replaced with teams of experts. But field work still involves digging—and danger.

As a young student, Dr. Juris Zarins got a summer job working for a museum as a "shovel bum" excavating sites in South Dakota. That job captivated his interest in archaeology, a field in which, he says, "nothing is ever boring." In his career as an archaeologist, Dr. Zarins often found himself working in interesting desert regions, including Mesopotamia and Egypt. In the following interview, he talks about his work.

Dr. Zarins takes notes in the field.

Q: What was the scariest thing that ever happened in your work?

A: *Dangerous* is certainly a term we could use in desert work. Going into the desert without careful preparation and sufficient supplies is very dangerous. Breaking down in the desert with little water could mean death.

Getting lost is another real concern. In the great Empty Quarter, a desert region in the southeastern interior of the Arabian Peninsula, the dunes are 600 feet (180 meters) high, and it is easy to lose one's way without navigational equipment. We also have to watch out for vipers—very dangerous snakes—when we are at a site. Putting your hands in dark places where snakes and scorpions can attack is really scary!

Mostly, though, I consider work in the desert to be adventurous, because we discover remote, abandoned sites that have sometimes been unseen for hundreds or thousands of years."

Q: How do you choose projects?

A: I answer three questions: First, will we receive permission to work on a site from the government of a country? Second, can we obtain the financial support for the project? And last, will we be able to interest others in helping us?

I started off working in Arabia, a peninsula surrounded by all sorts of interesting places like the Red Sea, Mesopotamia, and Iran and interesting people like the Sumerians, Egyptians, nomads, and Yemenis. Being there led me to many other places and people that have become the focus for other projects.

Q: Where do you work?

A: I always find myself in desert areas, but they can look very different. Some are rocky or hilly or have large areas of dunes. Some desert areas are coastal or near ancient springs. We get to a site by four-wheel-drive vehicles and then we walk, walk, walk.

You cannot see anything if you do not walk. I generally avoid going to huge dune areas by myself. I make sure that we have several vehicles and plenty of gas and water.

Dr. Juris Zarins directs a dig at the remains of Ubar, in the Middle Eastern country of Oman. Known as the Lost City, Ubar was mentioned in texts such as *The Arabian Nights*, but nobody knew its location until recently.

Q: What is a normal working day like for you?

A: A normal working day consists of getting up early, getting all the gear together, readying the cars, and checking equipment. Sometimes we drive a long way, forget something essential, like water, and have to go back. We eat a pack lunch in the field and then work until 4 or 5 p.m. In the Middle East, we primarily work during the winter. After supper we wash, look at artifacts, write about our work that day, then take a break and go to bed early. Usually, we have little or no artificial light to work by, so we have to work during the day.

Q: What is the hardest part of your work?

A: The hardest part of my work is being lonely. The days are long, and I miss my family, teaching school, and my friends. I am a sports nut. I like to play basketball and tennis and watch all sorts of sports on television, so I miss that very much when I am in the field.

WHY IT MATTERS TODAY

To collect information about the past, archaeologists like Dr. Zarins study and work for years. Their jobs are filled with adventure and the excitement of discovery, but they also have to work hard to interpret their findings. Because of their efforts, we continue to learn interesting and important things about ancient cultures.

The Mummy

Hunter & Mr. X

Dr. Hawass (seated left) supervises workers using ropes to pull aside the heavy lid of a sarcophagus, the stone coffin that holds a mummy case.

Of all the discoveries of the ancient past, the one that holds the most fascination for modern people is the Egyptian mummy. Today, archaeologists use new technologies to study ancient mummies. Dr. Zahi Hawass, director general of the Giza pyramids in Egypt, describes his work with mummies.

May I introduce you to a very old friend of mine? I call him Mr. X, and he's about 2,000 years old. My name is Zahi Hawass. In my work, I deal with the legacy of the ancient world nearly every day. But Mr. X was, and is, someone special. He's a mummy.

We found him in 1999, at an archaeological site in the Egyptian oasis town of Bahariya (bah–hah–REE–yah) —225 miles (360 kilometers) from the pyramids at Giza, near Cairo. We don't know what his real name was, so he's just Mr. X. (When I first excavated Mr. X, I called him Mr. or Mrs. X because I did not know if he was a man or a woman. X-rays later confirmed that he was male.) When he died, at about age 40, his body was neatly wrapped in linen bandages that were soaked in resin, a liquid substance that forms a hard coating when it dries. He was then buried in a niche, or compartment, in a honeycomb of underground tombs.

Mummies Everywhere!

This city of the dead sat undisturbed for centuries. Then in 1996, a passing donkey stumbled into a hole. As the donkey's owner worked to free its hoof, he saw a flash of gold in the sand below. It turns out that the donkey had punched a hole in the roof of a long-buried tomb. My archaeological team was called immediately.

What we found were mummies—more than have ever been found in one place before. The mummies of Bahariya are different from King Tut and other classic Egyptian mummies you may know. These are not anywhere near as old, and they weren't the remains of wealthy people.

In early Egypt, mummification was once just for royalty; it was a very expensive process. People believed that preserving a body would give the dead person everlasting life. By Mr. X's time, everyone wanted a chance at the afterlife. This cemetery was where many of the people who lived at the Bahariya oasis were entombed during the time when Greeks and Romans ruled Egypt. This period lasted from 332 B.C. until the fourth century A.D.

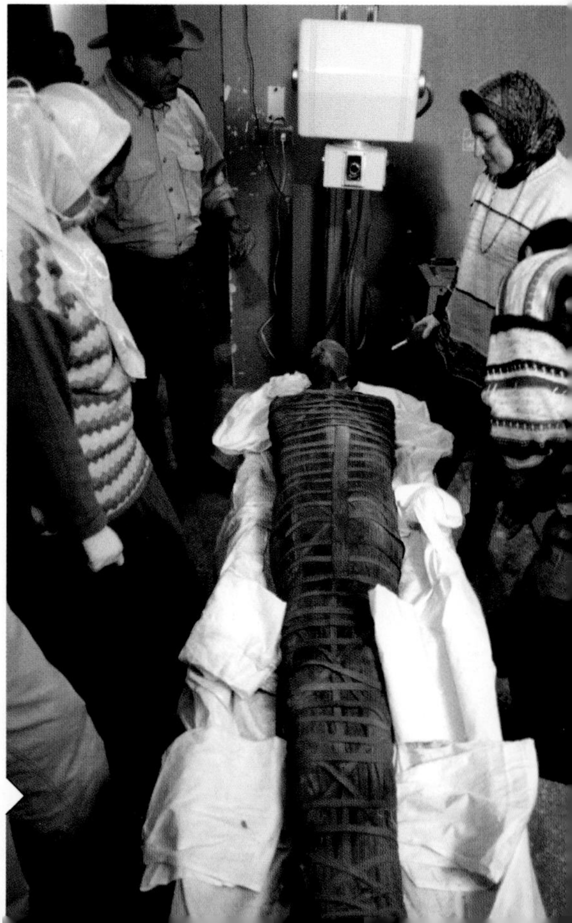

Egypt expert Zahi Hawass (with hat) helps his team study a pyramid worker's mummy.

Mr. X Goes to the Lab

To learn more about the mummies, we needed to move one to a laboratory to be x-rayed. I prefer not to move mummies from their resting places, but I chose Mr. X for the tests. He was in excellent condition and could be transported more easily than a mummy covered in gold. And since Mr. X was buried alone, no other mummies would be disturbed. We carefully removed the body and placed it in a wooden coffin.

First, I paused for a moment of silence. I requested Mr. X's forgiveness for disturbing him and silently asked that he teach us something of his world. Then I notified authorities that a truck bearing Mr. X was on its way to the lab, and the body should be received as that of an honored guest. I believe we should treat a mummy respectfully, as we would the body of a relative or friend. After all, that's the way we would want to be treated in similar circumstances!

X-ray Vision

We learned a great deal from Mr. X's x-rays. X-ray technology allows us to look at a mummy without disturbing his wrapping. We saw that Mr. X had a couple of teeth pulled during his lifetime. Before he was wrapped in bandages, a coin was placed in his hand—perhaps to pay his way into the afterlife.

The x-rays also showed that Mr. X had no major diseases at his death. I wondered then why he died so young. Later I x-rayed other mummies at Bahariya and found they had also died between 35 and 40 years of age. I had the bones analyzed and found they were full of iron. Too much iron can damage bones and body organs. I think iron may have poisoned their drinking water.

There is still much work to be done at the Bahariya tombs. Because these mummies were not buried with artifacts bearing their names, we cannot know if the ones we find buried together are related. Soon, I hope we can sample their DNA, from a bit of hair or fingernail, and know for certain if there are genetic links. It is always good to keep families together—in this life and for the next.

▶ *For more information about ancient Egypt, see pages 61–62.*

WHY IT MATTERS TODAY

X-rays and DNA tests allow us to study mummies without destroying them. Tests done on the Bahariya mummies show that Egyptians changed burial practices over time. Ordinary people, as well as royalty, could buy elaborate funeral procedures to prepare them for the afterlife. Much more work still awaits future mummy hunters.

The First Civilizations

This Overview provides a brief summary of the most important people, places, and events of ancient Mesopotamia and Egypt. Its purpose is to help you better understand the historical background of the articles in this book.

The First Farmers

The first farming villages arose in southwest Asia between 8000 and 5000 B.C. An increased food supply supported more people. Crafts such as pottery, weaving, and metalworking appeared. Trade began with other communities. About 3500 B.C., these communities moved into a new phase of human development—civilization.

What Is Civilization?

Historians consider people "civilized" when they have settled in one place and developed a complex society. Such societies have organized systems of government and law, and large-scale building projects, such as city walls, temples, palaces, and tombs.

Another feature of civilized communities is a system of writing to keep track of such things as taxes and laws.

Civilized societies also create a division of labor. Some people produce enough food for all. This frees the rest to engage in other work, such as trade, crafts, art, and education.

The first civilizations arose about 3500 B.C. in Mesopotamia, the fertile valley of the Tigris and Euphrates Rivers in what are now Syria and Iraq. At about the same time, civilization developed in Egypt along the Nile River.

Major Events

Before 3000 B.C.
Sumerians develop cuneiform

3100 B.C.
Schools established in Sumer

3000 B.C.

2700 B.C.
Old Kingdom begins

2550 B.C.
Great Pyramid built

2300 B.C.
Sargon unites Mesopotamia

Mesopotamia

Sunset on the Euphrates River

The Land Between the Rivers

The ancient region between the Tigris and Euphrates Rivers was called Mesopotamia (from Greek words meaning "land between the rivers"). The rivers begin in what is now Turkey and flow southeast to the Persian Gulf. In ancient times, they formed part of the Fertile Crescent. This was a region of rich farming and grazing land that extended from Mesopotamia to the Mediterranean coast.

Mesopotamia was a natural place for ancient peoples to settle. The Tigris and Euphrates provided the water necessary for farming. Their annual flooding left a fertile layer of mud and sand, or silt, which enriched the soil. However, early Mesopotamian farmers were never sure when the rivers would flood or how much water they would bring. These farmers could use the land only if they figured out a way to control the flow. This required cooperation among many people, which helped give rise to on of the first Mesopotamian civilizations, Sumer.

The Sumerians

The Sumerians may have migrated into southern Mesopotamia from mountains to the east. As they organized to control the flooding of the Tigris and Euphrates, their farming settlements began to grow larger and more complex. By about 3500 B.C., some of these settlements had become cities. However, the Sumerian cities rarely came together to form a single country. Instead, each was a city-state with its own government that ruled the surrounding region.

After 2000 B.C.
oic of Gilgamesh written

1750 B.C.
Hammurabi's Code

1304 B.C.
Ramses II becomes pharaoh

1075 B.C.
New Kingdom ends

:000 B.C. — 1000 B.C.

Bronze head of Sargon

Sumerian Civilization

The Sumerians created beautiful bronze artwork and understood mathematics. They counted by 10s, but also by 60s. They divided the circle into 360 degrees, the hour into 60 minutes, and the minute into 60 seconds. As their trade increased, they needed a way to keep records. So they invented a writing system based on pictograms drawn on clay tablets. Over time, these simple pictures developed into a complex wedge-shaped script called cuneiform.

As time passed, the Sumerians used their writing system to record literature. Some of this literature told stories of their early heroes and kings. The most famous of these stories dealt with the adventures of Gilgamesh, a legendary king of the Sumerian city of Uruk. Sumerian literature also included myths, hymns to their gods, love songs, and collections of proverbs.

Sargon

Between 3000 and 2000 B.C., migrants were drawn to Mesopotamia from the surrounding deserts. In about 2300 B.C., one of these people, a great military leader known as Sargon, conquered the city-states of southern Mesopotamia and united them into the first empire. Sargon extended his rule as far as what is now northern Syria, southern Turkey, and western Iran. Sargon ruled for 56 years, but his empire grew so large that it was difficult to control. After the death of his successor and grandson, Naram-Sin, the empire quickly collapsed following raids by a mountain people from the northeast.

Hammurabi

In about 2000 B.C., another group of invaders entered Mesopotamia from the northwest. They settled in the city of Babylon on the Euphrates River. In about 1790 B.C., their ruler Hammurabi, came to the throne. He reunited Mesopotamia into the first Babylonian Empire. Hammurabi is best known for his collection of law codes that covered everything from agriculture and trade to marriage, divorce, and even physician's fees. Hammurabi reigned for 40 years, but as with Sargon, his empire soon fell apart.

Egypt

Red Land and Black Land

The geography of the Nile Valley in northeast Africa shaped ancient Egyptian civilization. The annual flooding of the Nile enriched Egypt's soil with a rich layer of silt. This was the fertile "Black Land" where Egyptian civilization arose. The surrounding deserts and mountains were the "Red Land." For a long time, these harsh regions helped protect the Egyptians from invasion.

Between 4000 and 3000 B.C., the organization needed to dig and maintain irrigation canals helped the Egyptians develop the beginnings of civilization. By 3000 B.C., the villages of northern and southern Egypt—known as Lower and Upper Egypt—had been united into a single kingdom.

The Pyramid Age

Egypt's rulers were known as pharaohs, a title meaning "great house" or "palace." The ancient Egyptians viewed the pharaohs as living gods. When the pharaohs died, the Egyptians buried them in tombs attached to temples. As time passed, these tombs took the form of huge pyramids. The climax of the Pyramid Age came about 2550 B.C. with the construction of the Great Pyramid as a tomb for the pharaoh Khufu.

Mummy lying on a lion-shaped funerary bed guarded by gods

A complicated process of preservation prepared a pharaoh's body for the afterlife. Deep inside the pyramid, the walls of the burial chambers were covered with scenes of judgment by the gods or passages from the *Book of the Dead*. This was a collection of magic spells that protected and aided the pharaoh on the journey to the afterlife. Food, furniture, weapons, and ornaments were buried with the dead for use when they reached the afterlife.

Old and Middle Kingdoms

In the history of ancient Egypt, periods of strong rulers alternated with eras of disorder. The first great period of Egyptian history, called the Old Kingdom, began about 2700 B.C. By 2130 B.C., the Old Kingdom pharaohs had grown weak, and famine and civil war brought about the end of their rule. For nearly 200 years, rival leaders fought one another for control of Egypt.

About 1975 B.C., a strong line of pharaohs from the city of Thebes reunited the country. This began the second great period of Egyptian history, called the Middle Kingdom. For more than 300 years, Egypt was peaceful and well governed.

The pharaohs of the Middle Kingdom built great irrigation projects to control the Nile and began the greatest temple of all time, the Temple of Amun at Karnak. Egyptian ships traveled up and down the Nile to trade for gold and copper. There were great achievements in art, architecture, and literature.

In about 1630 B.C., parts of Upper Egypt fell to the Hyksos, a people who lived nearby. The invaders fought from horse-drawn war chariots and with bronze weapons. The tactics and weapons of the Hyksos were superior to anything used by the Egyptian army. The Hyksos invasion ended the Middle Kingdom.

Queen Nefertiti of Egypt

The New Kingdom

For nearly 100 years, the Hyksos ruled much of Egypt. Then about 1550 B.C., new pharaohs from Thebes adopted the tactics and weapons of the Hyksos. The Egyptians created a strong army and drove out the invaders. This began the last great period of Egyptian history, known as the New Kingdom.

The pharaohs of the New Kingdom now looked to expand Egypt beyond its ancient borders. The greatest of these empire builders, the pharaoh Thutmose III, invaded parts of Asia and extended Egyptian rule to the Euphrates.

The Egyptian empire began to decline when Amenhotep became pharaoh in 1353 B.C. and ruled with his wife, Queen Nefertiti. He replaced the old gods with one god, Aten, the sun disk. He changed his name to Akhenaten ("It is well with Aten") and had the names and faces of the old gods removed from tombs and monuments. He also moved the capital away from Thebes, angering the powerful priests.

His successor, Tutankhamen, restored the old gods. His lavish burial demonstrates the richness of the pharaoh's life during his brief ten-year reign. Ramses II, who reigned from 1304–1237 B.C., regained part of the territory that was lost by previous pharaohs. But Egypt's empire would never regain its earlier glory.

GLOSSARY

archaeologist a scientist who studies the remains of peoples and cultures of the past

civil laws laws covering noncriminal matters such as marriage and business contracts

cuneiform the wedge-shaped script of the ancient Sumerians

decipher decode; read or interpret something

delta the land at a river's mouth

embalmer a person who uses special methods to preserve a dead body from decay

excavate to dig out or remove soil from an area to find remains

expedition a trip taken with a definite purpose, such as scientific discovery

Fertile Crescent a region of rich farming and grazing land that extended from Mesopotamia to the Mediterranean coast

hieroglyphs the picture writing of the ancient Egyptians

mummy a human body preserved from decay

papyrus a reed from which the ancient Egyptians made paper

pharaoh a ruler of ancient Egypt

pictogram a picture used to represent a thing

scribe a person who copies documents by hand

silt the fertile layer of mud and sand left by a flooding river

stylus a sharp, pointed tool for writing

tablet house a school for scribes in ancient Sumer

The Egyptian pharaoh Mycerinus standing between two goddesses

INDEX

Akhenaten 62
archaeologists 8–9, 10–15, 18, 26, 34–36, 46–57, 63
art 46–49, 60, 62
Babylon 7, 60
Bahariya 54–57
Book of the Dead 42–43, 61
city-state 59–60
cuneiform 13–15, 17–18, 58, 60, 63
education 16–19
Egypt 4–5, 8–9, 15, 28–45, 51, 54–57, 61–63
embalmers 44–45, 63
Euphrates River 4, 6–7, 22, 58–60
excavate 8, 46, 48, 56, 63
farming 6, 30–31, 58–59, 61
Fertile Crescent 6, 59, 63
Gilgamesh 20–23, 59, 60
Giza 33–37, 54–55
government 7, 18, 31, 59–60
Hammurabi 7, 25–27, 59–60
Hawass, Zahi 54–57
hieroglyphs 15, 37, 63
law 7–9, 18, 24–27, 60
literature 8, 21–23, 60, 62
Mesopotamia 4, 6, 8–9, 13, 18, 21, 25, 51, 59–60
mummies 37, 45, 54–57, 63
Nile River 4–5, 8, 28–31, 58, 61–62
papyrus 30, 63
pharaohs 34–35, 38–39, 42–45, 61–63
pictogram 14, 63
pyramids 5, 7, 32–37, 43, 61
Rawlinson, Henry 10–13
religion 8, 40–45, 61–62
Rock of Behistun 12–13, 15
Rosetta Stone 15
scribes 16–19
silt 30, 61, 63
Sumerians 2, 6–10, 14–15–19, 22, 48–49, 59–60, 63
tablet house 16–19
Tigris River 4, 6, 58–59
trade 31, 58, 60
transportation 8, 31
Ur 2, 9, 46–49
Uruk 22–23
Woolley, Leonard 46–49
writing 10–19, 30, 58, 60
Zarins, Juris 50–53

Shell plaque with two goats from Queen Puabi's grave in the Sumerian city of Ur